HEY, THANKS

A GUIDED GRATITUDE JOURNAL

EM&
FRIENDS

I, ————————————,
HEREBY GRANT MYSELF FULL PERMISSION

to become the kind of person who not only **owns** a journal, but also the kind of person who **writes** in a journal. I give myself permission to not hold back for any excuse disguised as a "reason," like not having a cool pen with me or not liking the way my handwriting looks. I understand that my private thoughts and feelings are valid and don't permanently define me. I know that as a human being, I am capable of changing my mind and surprising myself. I give myself permission to let go of resentments, fears, and confusion. I can invite peace, encouragement, and forward momentum into my life. Or not. I get to decide what I journal about. Yay.

THERE IS NO WRONG WAY to KEEP A JOURNAL.

Signed: ————————————— Date:—————

HOW to USE this JOURNAL:

Hello! We are so glad you found your way to this journal. It was created with you in mind. The practice of gratitude, and all it entails, is a very personal experience, and it's different for everyone. As you start your practice, please give yourself permission to feel whatever you feel and to accept whatever may come up for you.

We also want you to understand that gratitude can be found anywhere and in anything. It's not just about being thankful for obvious things, like family, friends, or cute and affordable shoes. We encourage you to challenge yourself to find gratitude for the most mundane things you can think of, as well as the big, obvious circumstances that cause you to feel thankful.

Here are some ideas to keep in mind as you begin to practice gratitude:

Nothing is too small to be grateful for. The electricity providing you with the light to read these pages, having a pen you love to write with, the clean air you're breathing—gratitude can be found everywhere. Did you take a hot shower today? Did you hear a bird sing? Are you in your favorite stretchy pants? Are you at inbox zero?

These small details are easily taken for granted, but are also all opportunities to notice and practice gratitude.

Circumstances don't have to impact you directly for you to feel gratitude. When nothing seems to be going right for you, focusing on what is going right for others can turn your mood around. Picture all the animals that are being adopted today, or all the people who reached their destinations safely. Everyone around the world who looked up at the stars and felt a sense of wonder. Even when you can't see something to be grateful for, you can imagine all of the things happening in the world that are beautiful and special in someone else's reality.

You don't have to justify your gratitude. Throughout this journal, we provide you with spaces to go wild with gratitude. We've provided you with suggested topics to help organize your lists by theme, and we hope you dive deep into them. Be as general or specific as you like. For example, if you were filling in the "friends" section, you might write: "Jane's laughter always makes me laugh." Or it might be as simple as: "The way my friends show up for me."

You don't need to have this journal with you to strengthen your gratitude muscle. Challenge yourself to experience gratitude in the moment, wherever you are. Next time you're on the bus, or at a red light, look around you. Can you appreciate someone's sense of style or the sweet face of the dog they're walking? Are you listening to great music? Do you see a tree? A flower? A heart-shaped rock? Simply by looking around your surroundings in any given moment, you can easily count at least 5 things (or more!) that make you grateful for where you are, right then, in that moment. Try this exercise every day, and notice how your general outlook improves each and every time you do it.

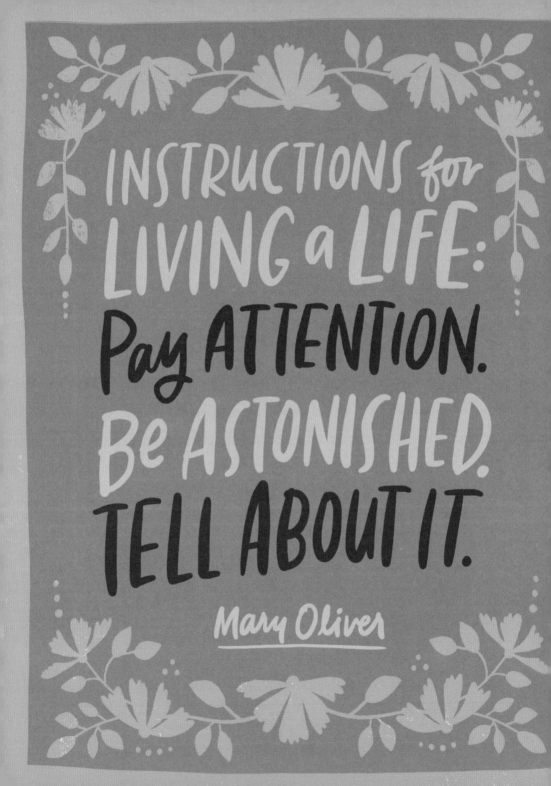

Write a thank-you note to someone in your life who was there for you when you needed them.

_____

_____

_____

_____

_____

_____

_____

_____

_____

_____

_____

_____

_____

TOPIC: _____

_____
_____
_____
_____
_____

TOPIC: _____

SOME POSSIBLE TOPICS:
•NATURE •FRIENDS •CAREER •AWARENESS •PETS •PHYSICAL OBJECTS (a.k.a. STUFF)
•HEALTH •FAMILY •PARTNER •LESSONS •PLACES •EXPERIENCES

TOPIC: _____

TOPIC: _____

GRA
EX

TOPIC: _____

_____

_____

_____

_____

DATE:

UDE
ON

TOPIC: ___

_____

_____

TOPIC: _____

INNER CHECK-IN

Date: _____

What's been on my mind lately:

What I've been enjoying:

What I've been struggling with:

NOTES AND OBSERVATIONS

SOME POSSIBLE TOPICS:

FRIENDS   CAREER   HEALTH   PHYSICAL OBJECTS (a.k.a. STUFF)
FAMILY   PARTNER   AWARENESS   EXPERIENCES
PETS   NATURE   LESSONS   PLACES

GRATITUDE List

DATE: _____

TOPIC: _____

TOPIC: _____

TOPIC: _____

TOPIC: _____

What qualities do you most appreciate about your favorite people, and why?

_____

_____

_____

_____

_____

_____

_____

_____

_____

_____

_____

_____

_____

What are some things which cause you to feel gratitude daily?
Or, what regular occurrences in your life COULD cause
you to feel gratitude daily?

TOPIC: _____

_____

_____

_____

_____

_____

TOPIC: _____

SOME POSSIBLE TOPICS:

• NATURE • FRIENDS • CAREER • AWARENESS • PETS • PHYSICAL OBJECTS (a.k.a. STUFF)
• HEALTH • FAMILY • PARTNER • LESSONS • PLACES • EXPERIENCES

TOPIC: _____

TOPIC: _____

TOPIC: _____

GR
EX

TOPIC: _____ _____

DATE: ____

DE
ON

TOPIC: _____ _____

TOPIC: _____ _____

INNER CHECK-IN

Date: _____

What's been on my mind lately:

What I've been enjoying:

What I've been struggling with:

FRIENDS   CAREER   HEALTH   PHYSICAL OBJECTS (a.k.a. STUFF)
FAMILY   PARTNER   AWARENESS EXPERIENCES
PETS   NATURE   LESSONS   PLACES

TOPIC:

TOPIC:

TOPIC:

TOPIC:

TOPIC:

GRATITUDE
List
DATE

GRATITUDE List

DATE:_____.

TOPIC:_____

TOPIC:_____

TOPIC:_____

TOPIC:_____

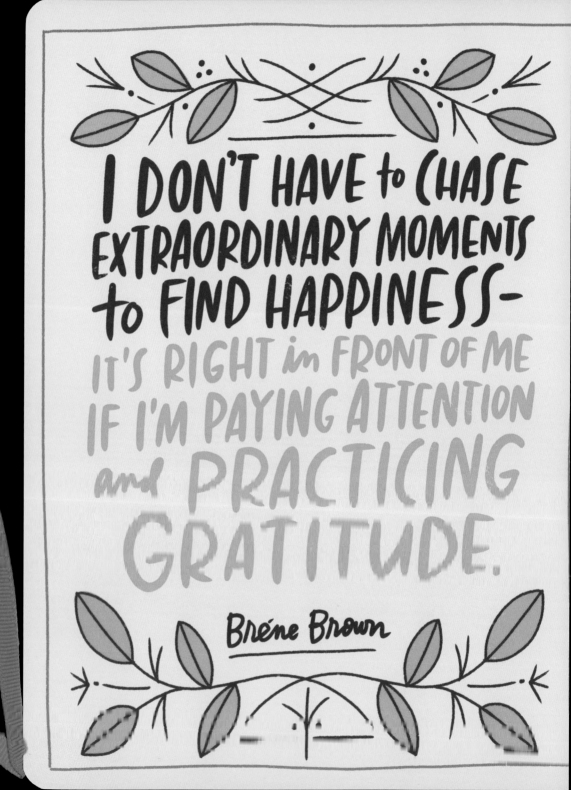

It's possible to feel gratitude and joy for things you haven't experienced. What are some of the wonders of the world that make you happy just because they exist?

_____

_____

_____

_____

_____

_____

_____

_____

_____

_____

_____

_____

_____

TOPIC: _____

_____

_____

_____

_____

_____

TOPIC: _____

TOPIC: _____

GRA
EX

TOPIC: _____

_____

_____

_____

_____

TOPIC: _____

TOPIC: _____
_____
_____
_____
_____

TOPIC: _____

DATE:
[   ]

UDE
ON

TOPIC: _____

_____
_____
_____

TOPIC: _____

INNER CHECK-IN

Date: _____

What's been on my mind lately:

What I've been working on:

What I have the opportunity to do differently:

NOTES AND OBSERVATIONS

SOME POSSIBLE TOPICS:

FRIENDS   CAREER   HEALTH   PHYSICAL OBJECTS (a.k.a. STUFF)
FAMILY   PARTNER   AWARENESS   EXPERIENCES
PETS   NATURE   LESSONS   PLACES

TOPIC:

TOPIC:

TOPIC:

TOPIC:

TOPIC:

GRATITUDE List

DATE

GRATITUDE List

DATE:_____.

TOPIC: _____

TOPIC: _____

TOPIC: _____

TOPIC: _____

What places have you traveled to or visited that brought
you experiences and opportunities you are thankful for?
Describe them here:

_____

_____

_____

_____

_____

_____

_____

_____

_____

_____

_____

_____

_____

Write a letter to your future self, expressing gratitude for things that haven't happened yet, but you hope or believe will happen. Write the letter as if all these things have taken place.

_____

_____

_____

_____

_____

_____

_____

_____

_____

_____

_____

_____

_____

_____

_____

_____

_____

_____

_____

_____

_____

SOME POSSIBLE TOPICS:

• NATURE   • FRIENDS   • CAREER   • AWARENESS   • PETS   • PHYSICAL OBJECTS (a.k.a. STUFF)
• HEALTH   • FAMILY   • PARTNER • LESSONS   • PLACES • EXPERIENCES

TOPIC: _____

TOPIC: _____

TOPIC: _____

TOPIC: _____

GR
EX

PIC: _____

_____

_____

_____

_____

IDE
N

PIC: _____

INNER CHECK-IN

Date: _____

What's been on my mind lately:

What I've been working on:

What I have the opportunity to do differently:

NOTES AND OBSERVATIONS

FRIENDS   CAREER   HEALTH   PHYSICAL OBJECTS (a.k.a. STUFF)
FAMILY   PARTNER   AWARENESS   EXPERIENCES
PETS   NATURE   LESSONS   PLACES

GRATITUDE List

DATE:_____.

TOPIC: _____

TOPIC: _____

TOPIC: _____

TOPIC: _____

TOPIC: _____

_____

_____

_____

_____

_____

SOME POSSIBLE TOPICS:
•NATURE •FRIENDS •CAREER •AWARENESS •PETS •PHYSICAL OBJECTS (a.k.a. STUFF)
•HEALTH •FAMILY •PARTNER •LESSONS •PLACES •EXPERIENCES

TOPIC: _____

TOPIC: _____

GRA
EX

TOPIC: _____

TOPIC: _____

TOPIC: _____

TOPIC: _____

DATE:

IDE
N

PIC: _____

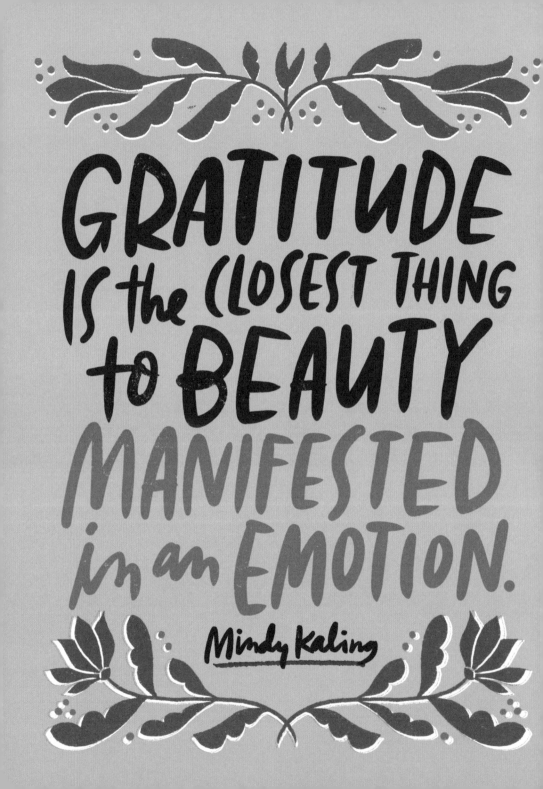

Write a thank-you letter to your physical body.
Express gratitude for all it allows you to do, and what gifts
it gives you. Consider both your internal physical body and
your outward-facing physical self.

_____

_____

_____

_____

_____

_____

_____

_____

_____

_____

_____

_____

_____

_____

_____

TOPIC: _____

_____
_____
_____
_____
_____

TOPIC: _____

TOPIC: _____

SOME POSSIBLE TOPICS:

- NATURE
- HEALTH
- FRIENDS
- FAMILY
- CAREER
- PARTNER
- AWARENESS
- LESSONS
- PETS
- PLACES
- PHYSICAL OBJECTS (a.k.a. STUFF)
- EXPERIENCES

TOPIC: _____

_____
_____
_____
_____

TOPIC: _____

TOPIC: _____

TOPIC: _____

DATE: _____

TOPIC: _____

PIC: _____

INNER CHECK-IN

Date: _____

What's been on my mind lately:

What I've really enjoyed recently:

What I'm looking forward to:

NOTES AND OBSERVATIONS

SOME POSSIBLE TOPICS:

FRIENDS   CAREER   HEALTH   PHYSICAL OBJECTS (a.k.a. STUFF)
FAMILY   PARTNER   AWARENESS   EXPERIENCES
PETS   NATURE   LESSONS   PLACES

TOPIC:

TOPIC:

TOPIC:

TOPIC:

TOPIC:

GRATITUDE List

DATE

GRATITUDE List

DATE:_____

TOPIC: _____   TOPIC: _____

TOPIC: _____   TOPIC: _____

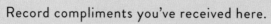

Record compliments you've received here.

What are five things you love about yourself that are unique to you? Why do you love them?

_____

_____

_____

_____

_____

_____

_____

_____

_____

_____

_____

_____

_____

_____

_____

_____

_____

_____

TOPIC: _____

_____

_____

_____

_____

_____

_____

TOPIC: _____

SOME POSSIBLE TOPICS:
• NATURE   • FRIENDS   • CAREER   • AWARENESS   • PETS   • PHYSICAL OBJECTS (a.k.a. STUFF)
• HEALTH   • FAMILY   • PARTNER   • LESSONS   • PLACES   • EXPERIENCES

GR
EX

TOPIC: _____

_____

_____

_____

TOPIC: _____

TOPIC: _____

TOPIC: _____

TOPIC: _____

DATE: _____

TOPIC: _____

INNER CHECK-IN

Date: _____

What's been on my mind lately:

What I've really enjoyed recently:

What I'm looking forward to:

NOTES AND OBSERVATIONS

SOME POSSIBLE TOPICS:

FRIENDS   CAREER   HEALTH   PHYSICAL OBJECTS (a.k.a. STUFF)
FAMILY   PARTNER   AWARENESS   EXPERIENCES
PETS   NATURE   LESSONS   PLACES

TOPIC:

TOPIC:

TOPIC:

TOPIC:

TOPIC:

GRATITUDE List

DATE

GRATITUDE List

DATE: _____

TOPIC: _____   TOPIC: _____

TOPIC: _____   TOPIC: _____

TOPIC: _____

TOPIC: _____

TOPIC: _____

TOPIC: _____

GRA
EX

TOPIC: _____

PIC: _____

DATE:
[   ]

TOPIC: _____

PIC: _____

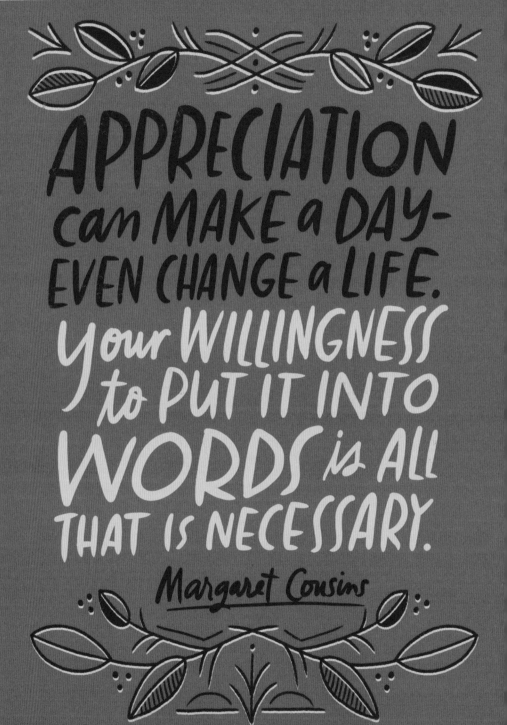

APPRECIATION can MAKE a DAY—EVEN CHANGE a LIFE. Your WILLINGNESS to PUT IT INTO WORDS is ALL THAT IS NECESSARY.

Margaret Cousins

Keep track of everything you're grateful for in a typical day. Don't forget the small things, like "I'm thankful for getting to where I needed to go safely."

_____

_____

_____

_____

_____

_____

_____

_____

_____

_____

_____

_____

_____

_____

_____

_____

_____

_____

_____

_____

TOPIC: _____

SOME POSSIBLE TOPICS:
- NATURE · FRIENDS · CAREER · AWARENESS · PETS · PHYSICAL OBJECTS (a.k.a. STUFF)
- HEALTH · FAMILY · PARTNER · LESSONS · PLACES · EXPERIENCES

GR
EX

TOPIC: _____

_____

_____

_____

TOPIC: _____

PIC: _____

TOPIC: _____

DATE:

DE
N

TOPIC: _____

PIC: _____

INNER CHECK-IN

Date: _____

What's been on my mind lately:

What I'm ready to change:

What I'm ready to let go of:

NOTES AND OBSERVATIONS

SOME POSSIBLE TOPICS:

FRIENDS   CAREER   HEALTH   PHYSICAL OBJECTS (a.k.a. STUFF)
FAMILY   PARTNER   AWARENESS   EXPERIENCES
PETS   NATURE   LESSONS   PLACES

GRATITUDE List

DATE

GRATITUDE List

DATE:_____

TOPIC: _____

TOPIC: _____

TOPIC: _____

TOPIC: _____

Try to express as much gratitude as you can this week.
Compliment strangers, thank people who help you in shops,
find things to express thankfulness for to people you see
every day. Record your experiences here.

_____

_____

_____

_____

_____

_____

_____

_____

_____

_____

_____

_____

_____

_____

_____

How does gratitude make you feel in your body? How does practicing gratitude lift you up? What benefits do you notice from expressing gratitude?

- NATURE
- HEALTH
- FRIENDS
- FAMILY
- CAREER
- PARTNER
- AWARENESS
- LESSONS
- PETS
- PLACES
- PHYSICAL OBJECTS (a.k.a. STUFF)
- EXPERIENCES

TOPIC: _____

_____

_____

_____

_____

_____

TOPIC: _____

TOPIC: _____

_____

_____

_____

_____

_____

TOPIC: _____

GR
EX

TOPIC: _____

TOPIC: _____

DATE:

IDE
N

TOPIC: _____

INNER CHECK-IN

Date: _____

What's been on my mind lately:

What I'm ready to change:

What I'm ready to let go of:

NOTES AND OBSERVATIONS

SOME POSSIBLE TOPICS:

FRIENDS   CAREER   HEALTH   PHYSICAL OBJECTS (a.k.a. STUFF)
FAMILY   PARTNER   AWARENESS   EXPERIENCES
PETS   NATURE   LESSONS   PLACES

TOPIC:

TOPIC:

TOPIC:

TOPIC:

TOPIC:

GRATITUDE List

DATE

GRATITUDE List

DATE: _____

TOPIC: _____

TOPIC: _____

TOPIC: _____

TOPIC: _____

TOPIC: _____

_____

_____

_____

_____

_____

TOPIC: _____

SOME POSSIBLE TOPICS:

• NATURE • FRIENDS • CAREER • AWARENESS • PETS • PHYSICAL OBJECTS (a.k.a. STUFF)
• HEALTH • FAMILY • PARTNER • LESSONS • PLACES • EXPERIENCES

GR
EX

TOPIC: _____

TOPIC: _____ _____

TOPIC: _____

TOPIC: _____

DATE: _____

IDE
N

TOPIC: _____

TOPIC: _____

BE THANKFUL
FOR WHAT YOU HAVE;
YOU'LL END UP HAVING MORE.
IF YOU CONCENTRATE
ON WHAT YOU DON'T HAVE,
YOU NEVER, EVER
HAVE ENOUGH.

Oprah Winfrey

What goals have you been able to accomplish?
Who helped you along the way? How did you make your
own success possible?

_____

_____

_____

_____

_____

_____

_____

_____

_____

_____

_____

_____

_____

_____

TOPIC: _____
_____
_____
_____
_____
_____
_____

TOPIC: _____

SOME POSSIBLE TOPICS:

- NATURE
- HEALTH
- FRIENDS
- FAMILY
- CAREER
- PARTNER
- AWARENESS
- LESSONS
- PETS
- PLACES
- PHYSICAL OBJECTS (a.k.a. STUFF)
- EXPERIENCES

TOPIC: _____

GR
EX

TOPIC: _____

_____
_____
_____
_____
_____
_____

TOPIC: _____

TOPIC: _____

TOPIC: _____

DATE: _____

TOPIC: _____

INNER CHECK-IN

Date: _____

What's been on my mind lately:

What I've been enjoying:

What I've been struggling with:

NOTES AND OBSERVATIONS

SOME POSSIBLE TOPICS:

FRIENDS CAREER HEALTH   PHYSICAL OBJECTS (a.k.a. STUFF)
FAMILY   PARTNER AWARENESS   EXPERIENCES
PETS   NATURE LESSONS   PLACES

GRATITUDE List

DATE:_____.

TOPIC: _____

TOPIC: _____

TOPIC: _____

TOPIC: _____

Recall a past disappointment. Looking back now at the way things worked out in the end, what benefits came out of the situation that you're grateful for?

_____

_____

_____

_____

_____

_____

_____

_____

_____

_____

_____

_____

_____

Write a list of challenges you've faced and how
you overcame them.

_____

_____

_____

_____

_____

_____

_____

_____

_____

_____

_____

_____

_____

TOPIC: _____

_____

_____

_____

_____

_____

_____

TOPIC: __

- NATURE
- HEALTH
- FRIENDS
- FAMILY
- CAREER
- PARTNER
- AWARENESS
- LESSONS
- PETS
- PLACES
- PHYSICAL OBJECTS (a.k.a. STUFF)
- EXPERIENCES

TOPIC: __

GR
EX

TOPIC: __

_____

_____

_____

_____

_____

TOPIC: _____

PIC: _____

TOPIC: _____

DATE:
[   ]
IDE
N

TOPIC: _____

PIC: _____

INNER CHECK-IN

Date: _____

What's been on my mind lately:

What I've been enjoying:

What I've been struggling with:

NOTES AND OBSERVATIONS

SOME POSSIBLE TOPICS:

FRIENDS   CAREER   HEALTH   PHYSICAL OBJECTS (a.k.a. STUFF)
FAMILY   PARTNER   AWARENESS   EXPERIENCES
PETS   NATURE   LESSONS   PLACES

TOPIC:

TOPIC:

TOPIC:

TOPIC:

TOPIC:

GRATITUDE List

DATE

GRATITUDE List

DATE:_____

TOPIC: _____

TOPIC: _____

TOPIC: _____

TOPIC: _____

TOPIC: _____

_____
_____
_____
_____
_____

TOPIC: _____

TOPIC: _____

GR
EX

SOME POSSIBLE TOPICS:

• NATURE   • FRIENDS   • CAREER   • AWARENESS   • PETS   • PHYSICAL OBJECTS (a.k.a. STUFF)
• HEALTH   • FAMILY   • PARTNER   • LESSONS   • PLACES   • EXPERIENCES

TOPIC: _____

TOPIC: _____

TOPIC: _____

DATE: _____

TOPIC: _____

TOPIC: _____

I TRY TO
START EVERY DAY
and
END EVERY DAY
By TAKING a MOMENT
TO BE GRATEFUL.

Olivia Wilde

What have you learned from family members that benefits you, and has informed how you live your life today? What's been passed on to you that you're grateful for?

_____

_____

_____

_____

_____

_____

_____

_____

_____

_____

_____

_____

_____

_____

_____

TOPIC: _____

_____

_____

_____

_____

_____

_____

TOPIC: ___

SOME POSSIBLE TOPICS:

- NATURE - FRIENDS - CAREER - AWARENESS - PETS - PHYSICAL OBJECTS (a.k.a. STUFF)
- HEALTH - FAMILY - PARTNER - LESSONS - PLACES - EXPERIENCES

TOPIC: ___

GR
E

TOPIC: _____

TOPIC: _____

TOPIC: _____

TOPIC: _____

DATE: _____

TOPIC: _____

INNER CHECK-IN

Date: _____

What's been on my mind lately:

What I've been working on:

What I have the opportunity to do differently:

NOTES AND OBSERVATIONS

SOME POSSIBLE TOPICS:

FRIENDS   CAREER   HEALTH   PHYSICAL OBJECTS (a.k.a. STUFF)
FAMILY   PARTNER   AWARENESS   EXPERIENCES
PETS   NATURE   LESSONS   PLACES

GRATITUDE List

DATE:_____.

OPIC: _____

TOPIC: _____

OPIC: _____

TOPIC: _____

What are three of your natural talents or abilities?
What do you love about them? How have they helped you out?

_____

_____

_____

_____

_____

_____

_____

_____

_____

_____

_____

_____

_____

_____

Sometimes, we feel grateful for the opportunity to help people we love—or random strangers! In what ways have you experienced this?

_____

_____

_____

_____

_____

_____

_____

_____

_____

_____

_____

_____

_____

_____

_____

_____

SOME POSSIBLE TOPICS:

- NATURE
- HEALTH
- FRIENDS
- FAMILY
- CAREER
- PARTNER
- AWARENESS
- LESSONS
- PETS
- PLACES
- PHYSICAL OBJECTS (a.k.a. STUFF)
- EXPERIENCES

TOPIC: _____

TOPIC: _____

TOPIC: _____

TOPIC: _____

GR
EX

TOPIC:

PIC: _____

DATE: [   ]

IDE
N

TOPIC:

PIC: _____

INNER CHECK-IN

Date: _____

What's been on my mind lately:

What I've been working on:

What I have the opportunity to do differently:

NOTES AND OBSERVATIONS

SOME POSSIBLE TOPICS:

FRIENDS   CAREER   HEALTH   PHYSICAL OBJECTS (a.ka. STUFF)
FAMILY   PARTNER   AWARENESS   EXPERIENCES
PETS   NATURE   LESSONS   PLACES

GRATITUDE List

DATE:_____

TOPIC: _____

TOPIC: _____

TOPIC: _____

TOPIC: _____

SOME POSSIBLE TOPICS:

- NATURE
- HEALTH
- FRIENDS
- FAMILY
- CAREER
- PARTNER
- AWARENESS
- LESSONS
- PETS
- PLACES
- PHYSICAL OBJECTS (a.k.a. STUFF)
- EXPERIENCES

TOPIC: _____

TOPIC:

TOPIC:

TOPIC: _____

GR
EX

PIC: _____

TOPIC: _____

DATE: _____

MDE
ON

TOPIC: _____

PIC: _____

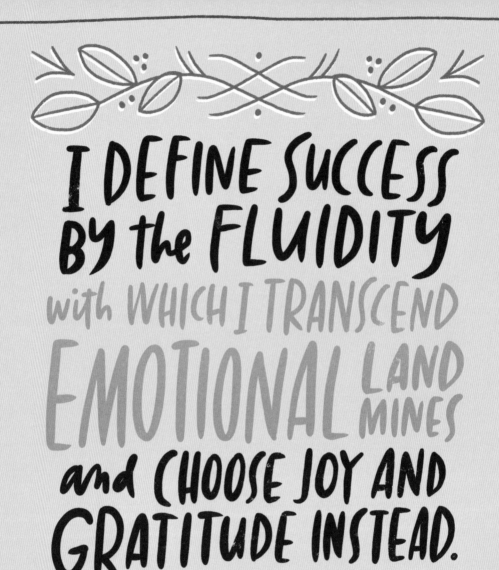

I DEFINE SUCCESS BY the FLUIDITY with WHICH I TRANSCEND EMOTIONAL LAND MINES and CHOOSE JOY AND GRATITUDE INSTEAD.

RuPaul Charles

Look around the room you're in. List all the things
you're grateful for, and why.

_____

_____

_____

_____

_____

_____

_____

_____

_____

_____

_____

_____

_____

TOPIC: _____
_____
_____
_____
_____
_____
_____

TOPIC: _____

SOME POSSIBLE TOPICS:

• NATURE • FRIENDS • CAREER • AWARENESS • PETS • PHYSICAL OBJECTS (a.k.a. STUFF)
• HEALTH • FAMILY • PARTNER • LESSONS • PLACES • EXPERIENCES

TOPIC: _____

TOPIC: _____

GR
E

TOPIC: _____

PIC: _____

DATE:

IDE
N

TOPIC: _____

PIC: _____

INNER CHECK-IN

Date: _____

What's been on my mind lately:

What I've really enjoyed recently:

What I'm looking forward to:

NOTES AND OBSERVATIONS

SOME POSSIBLE TOPICS:

FRIENDS CAREER   HEALTH   PHYSICAL OBJECTS (a.k.a. STUFF)
FAMILY   PARTNER AWARENESS   EXPERIENCES
PETS   NATURE   LESSONS   PLACES

TOPIC:

TOPIC:

TOPIC:

TOPIC:

TOPIC:

GRATITUDE List

DATE

GRATITUDE List

DATE:_____

TOPIC:_____

TOPIC:_____

TOPIC:_____

TOPIC:_____

What are some material gifts you've received that benefited you? Expand on them here.

What does kindness mean to you?
How do you show kindness? How do you receive it?

_____

_____

_____

_____

_____

_____

_____

_____

_____

_____

_____

_____

_____

TOPIC: _____

_____

_____

_____

_____

_____

TOPIC: ___

SOME POSSIBLE TOPICS:
• NATURE • FRIENDS • CAREER • AWARENESS • PETS • PHYSICAL OBJECTS (a.k.a. STUFF)
• HEALTH • FAMILY • PARTNER • LESSONS • PLACES • EXPERIENCES

TOPIC: ___

GR
EX

TOPIC: ___

TOPIC: _____

TOPIC: _____

TOPIC: _____

DATE: _____

IDE
ON

TOPIC: _____

PIC: _____

INNER CHECK-IN

Date: _____

What's been on my mind lately:

What I've really enjoyed recently:

What I'm looking forward to:

NOTES AND OBSERVATIONS

SOME POSSIBLE TOPICS:

FRIENDS   CAREER   HEALTH   PHYSICAL OBJECTS (a.ka. STUFF)
FAMILY   PARTNER   AWARENESS   EXPERIENCES
PETS   NATURE   LESSONS   PLACES

TOPIC:

TOPIC:

TOPIC:

TOPIC:

TOPIC:

GRATITUDE List

DATE

GRATITUDE List

DATE:_____

TOPIC: _____

TOPIC: _____

TOPIC: _____

TOPIC: _____

Choose three of these words, and then write about how
these themes show up in your life:

*Humor Kindness Love Adventure Satisfaction
Possibility Resilience Independence Generosity*

_____

_____

_____

_____

_____

_____

_____

_____

_____

_____

_____

_____

_____

TOPIC: _____

TOPIC: _____

SOME POSSIBLE TOPICS:

- NATURE   - FRIENDS   - CAREER   - AWARENESS   - PETS   - PHYSICAL OBJECTS (a.k.a. STUFF)
- HEALTH   - FAMILY   - PARTNER   - LESSONS   - PLACES   - EXPERIENCES

TOPIC: _____

TOPIC: _____

GR
EX

TOPIC: _____

TOPIC: _____

PIC: _____

DATE: [____]

TOPIC: _____

PIC: _____

INNER CHECK-IN

Date: _____

What's been on my mind lately:

What I'm ready to change:

What I'm ready to let go of:

NOTES AND OBSERVATIONS

SOME POSSIBLE TOPICS:

FRIENDS
FAMILY
PETS

CAREER
PARTNER
NATURE

HEALTH
AWARENESS
LESSONS

PHYSICAL OBJECTS (a.k.a. STUFF)
EXPERIENCES
PLACES

TOPIC:

TOPIC:

TOPIC:

TOPIC:

TOPIC:

GRATITUDE
List
DATE

GRATITUDE List

DATE:_____.

TOPIC: _____

TOPIC: _____

TOPIC: _____

TOPIC: _____

What are some of the biggest life lessons you've had to face? What little (or not-so-little!) hidden blessings did they come with?

_____

_____

_____

_____

_____

_____

_____

_____

_____

_____

_____

_____

_____

_____

What are some things about yourself you wish were
different? As things stand now, can you find reasons
to be grateful for where you're currently at?

_____

_____

_____

_____

_____

_____

_____

_____

_____

_____

_____

_____

_____

_____

_____

_____

TOPIC: _____

TOPIC: _____

TOPIC: _____

TOPIC: _____

GR
EX

OPIC: _____

DATE: _____

IDE
ON

TOPIC: _____

OPIC: _____

INNER CHECK-IN

Date: _____

What's been on my mind lately:

What I'm ready to change:

What I'm ready to let go of:

NOTES AND OBSERVATIONS

SOME POSSIBLE TOPICS:

FRIENDS   CAREER   HEALTH   PHYSICAL OBJECTS (a.k.a. STUFF)
FAMILY   PARTNER   AWARENESS   EXPERIENCES
PETS   NATURE   LESSONS   PLACES

TOPIC:

TOPIC:

TOPIC:

TOPIC:

TOPIC:

GRATITUDE List

DATE

GRATITUDE List

DATE:_____.

TOPIC: _____

TOPIC: _____

TOPIC: _____

TOPIC: _____

NOTES AND OBSERVATIONS

I ACTUALLY COMPLETED
A JOURNAL
Award

THIS AMAZING ACHIEVEMENT AWARD
IS HEREBY ISSUED to ME,

_____

FOR the MIGHTY TASK OF
ACTUALLY COMPLETING A JOURNAL.

I HONOR MYSELF and MY ACCOMPLISHMENT
on THIS ___ DAY OF _____, in the YEAR OF ____.

I AM A PERSON
WHO JOURNALS NOW.

_____
SIGNED